Unsolved Mysterie

D0454414

Water Monsters

Brian Innes

RSVP
**RAINTREE
Steck-Vaughn**
P U B L I S H E R S
A Steck-Vaughn Company

Austin, Texas

Developed by Brown Partworks
Editor: Lindsey Lowe
Designer: Joan Curtis

Raintree Steck-Vaughn Publishers Staff
Project Manager: Joyce Spicer
Editor: Pam Wells

Library of Congress Cataloging-in-Publication Data
Innes, Brian.
    Water monsters/by Brian Innes.
        p.   cm.—(Unsolved mysteries)
    Includes bibliographical references and index.
    Summary: Describes sightings of unidentified water creatures, including
the Biblical Leviathan, sea serpents, and the monsters supposedly inhabiting
various lakes.
    ISBN 0-8172-5479-X (Hardcover)
    ISBN 0-8172-4276-7 (Softcover)
    1. Marine animals—Juvenile literature. 2. Sea monsters—Juvenile literature.
[1. Sea monsters. 2. Monsters.] I. Title. II. Series: Innes, Brian. Unsolved
mysteries.
QL122.2.I56   1999
001.944—dc21   98-9353
                                                            CIP
                                                             AC
Printed and bound in the United States
2 3 4 5 6 7 8 9 0 WZ 02 01 00

Acknowledgments

Cover Norbert Wu/NHPA; **Page 5:** Charles
Walker Collection/Images Colour Library;
Page 6: Fortean Picture Library; **Page 7:** Stephen
Frink/Corbis; **Page 8:** Fortean Picture Library;
Page 9: Library of Congress/Corbis;
Page 11: Robert Le Serrec/Fortean Picture
Library; **Page 12:** James L. Amos/Corbis;
Pages 13 and 15: Fortean Picture Library;
Page 16: Kevin Schafer/Corbis; **Page 19:** Mary
Evans Picture Library; **Page 21:** Topham
Picturepoint; **Page 22:** Mary Evans Picture Library;
Page 23: Patrick Ward/Corbis; **Page 24:** Fortean
Picture Library; **Page 25:** Popperfoto;
Page 27: Nicholas Witchell/Fortean Picture
Library; **Page 29:** David Muench/Corbis;
Page 30: Fortean Picture Library; **Page 31:**
Kevin Morris/Corbis; **Page 33:** Hellin & Van
Ingen/NHPA; **Page 34:** Rene Dahinden/Fortean
Picture Library; **Page 37:** Rin Ergenbright/Corbis;
Page 38: Debbie Lee/Fortean Picture Library;
Page 39: Lars Thomas/Fortean Picture Library;
Page 41: Ivor Newby/Fortean Picture Library;
Page 43: Loren Coleman/Fortean Picture Library;
Page 44: Doug Perrine/Planet Earth Pictures;
Page 45: Pete Oxford/Planet Earth Pictures;
Page 46: Fortean Picture Library.

Contents

Creatures of the Deep

Many years ago people thought monsters lived in the oceans. Do any still lurk in the murky depths?

For centuries, sailors have told tales of giant sea serpents. They have seen them all over the world. One sea monster, called Leviathan, is mentioned five times in the Bible. It is described as "the twisting serpent, the dragon that is in the sea."

Many stories of Leviathan were collected by Olaus Magnus, a Swedish archbishop. He lived more than 400 years ago. He described the creature as black with a mane and shining eyes. It raised its head "on high like a pillar." He said it was 200 feet (60 m) long, and 20 feet (6 m) thick. It ate calves, lambs, and hogs. It would even drag men from boats.

A BEAST KNOWN FROM LEGENDS

In the 18th century this description was confirmed. A Danish ship dropped its anchor in calm waters off the coast of West Africa. The captain, Jean-Magnus Dens, decided it was a good time to scrape the ship's hull. Men were lowered over the side on planks to do this.

Suddenly a monster rose out of the sea. It had enormous arms. It pulled two sailors into the water. A third arm seized another sailor.

The legend of the sea monster Leviathan (opposite) struck terror in the hearts of sailors for many centuries.

4

"It raised its head 'on high like a pillar' . . . . It ate calves, lambs, and hogs. It would even drag men from boats."

His shipmates saved him by hacking through the monster's arm. The monster sank out of sight. The captain measured the piece of arm. It was 25 feet (7.5 m) long, and covered with suckers. He thought the whole arm must have been nearly 40 feet (12 m) long!

MONSTROUS SQUIDS

Pierre Denys de Montfort believed Captain Dens's story. He was a French expert on mollusks, animals with no backbone, usually living in a shell. He began to follow up every story he heard about giant squids. In the 1790s he went to Dunkirk, in northern France. A group of American whaling ships was based there. He met with Ben Johnson, one of the captains. Johnson told De Montfort that part of a squid arm had been found in a whale's mouth. The arm was 35 feet (10.5 m) long. De Montfort guessed the full length of the arm must have been nearly 80 feet (24 m).

Then they shared another story. The crew of a slave ship had been off the coast of West Africa. Suddenly a huge squid surfaced. The tips of its arms reached as high as the masts. It pulled the ship over. The crew prayed to St. Thomas. They managed to cut off the monster's arms and save themselves. As a thanksgiving, the

In 1861, the crew of the French gunboat Alecton tried to pull the body of an enormous squid on board, but failed.

6

It is no wonder that early seafarers thought the oceans were full of monsters. Just the eye of a giant squid can be as much as 18 inches (46 cm) wide!

crew hung a painting of the incident in St. Thomas's chapel at St. Malo in France.

De Montfort hurried to St. Malo to look at the painting. Later he described it to an artist. The artist made a picture from the description. De Montfort took the picture to Paris, the capital city of France. But none of the scientists in Paris believed the story. People laughed at De Montfort's ideas. The painting later disappeared. It has never been seen again.

PRIZE CATCHES

Some 60 to 70 years later, De Montfort's findings did not look so funny. On November 30, 1861, the French gunboat *Alecton* was near Tenerife, in the Canary Islands. The lookout spotted the body of a huge squid floating on the water. The ship's commander wanted to land it. After many attempts, the crew got a rope around the squid. They tried to pull it on board the ship. But the squid broke into pieces. Most fell back into the water and were washed away.

Later, dead and dying squids began to wash up on the coasts of Canada. The biggest one on record in Canada was found on November 2, 1878. Its body was over 20 feet (6 m) long. One of its arms was 35 feet (10.5 m) long. Its suckers were 4 inches (10 cm) across. Its eyes were 18 inches (46 cm) wide.

In the late 20th century a giant male pink squid was caught off the coast of Peru. It also had arms 35 feet (10.5 m) long. Its eyes were over 1 foot (30 cm) wide. Biologists worked out the size of the whole squid from the pieces. It would have been over 100 feet (30 m) long. In 1997 a report in the *New York Times* told of a giant female squid that had been captured off the coast of Australia. It was 50 feet (15 m) long. The giant squid certainly exists.

This etching of the Gloucester sea serpent became well-known after the monster was first seen in June 1815.

GIANT SNAKES

During the 18th and 19th centuries, many experienced naturalists kept an open mind about the existence of sea serpents. In the U.S., sea serpents were often spotted off the coast of New England. In June 1815, one was seen swimming rapidly through the water in Gloucester Bay, Massachusetts. It had a head like a horse and was dark brown. Its body was about 100 feet (30 m) long. It looked like a string of 30 to 40 humps, each the size of a barrel.

Judge Lonson Nash also said he saw the monster in Gloucester Bay. He led an investigation into all the sightings. This was organized by a group of New England scientists who studied living things. They decided the animal was a huge snake. They thought it had come to lay eggs on shore. No eggs were discovered, but two boys later found a creature. It was

"... it was 'just a black snake.' "

CHARLES-ALEXANDRE LESUEUR

3 feet (91 cm) long. It looked like a black snake, but it had humps on its back. Some thought it was a baby sea serpent. The biologists were excited. They named it *Scoliophis Atlanticus* (Atlantic Humped Snake). They cut it apart to examine it. But then a French zoologist, Charles-Alexandre Lesueur, looked at it. He said it was "just a black snake." Its spine had been deformed by injury or disease.

However, sightings of sea serpents continued. In 1820, the commander of the merchant ship *Lady Combermere* reported a serpent in the mid-Atlantic. It was 60 feet (18 m) long. In the 1830s, similar sightings of monsters were reported off Charleston, South Carolina, and Mahone Bay, Nova Scotia.

Most scientists laughed at such stories. However, reports of them have continued. Sea serpents are apparently still being sighted today.

Scientists in the 19th century laughed at reports of the existence of sea serpents. But does this 1906 photograph prove them right or wrong?

20th Century Sea Monsters

In the 20th century, photos finally proved the existence of sea monsters. Or did they?

Before the 1960s, no monsters had been photographed clearly. Then, in 1965, Robert Le Serrec astonished the world with color pictures (opposite) that he had taken in Australia. They appeared to show sea monsters.

Tales of strange creatures of the deep continued into the 20th century. Transatlantic passenger traffic was at its height during the 1920s and 1930s, and many people on cruises claimed to have seen sea monsters. There were also more reports of close-up sightings. There were even pictures to prove them!

CLOSE CONTACTS

For many years, a sea serpent had been seen in Chesapeake Bay, Maryland. Known locally as "Chessie," it became a film star in 1982. On May 21, Robert Frew and his wife, Karen, were entertaining guests at their home on Kent Island. Their home was near the north end of the vast bay. Around 7:00 P.M., they all saw Chessie. The sea serpent was in clear, shallow water about 200 yards (182 m) away. Robert grabbed his video camera. He began shooting film from an upper bedroom window.

The monster was moving up and down in the water. It was heading toward a party of swimmers. The Frews and their friends shouted. But the swimmers did not hear them. The swimmers did not notice the monster either. It dived

"It was shaped like an enormous tadpole. It had a big head, and a long, tapering body."

"Chessie" the sea serpent is said to lurk beneath the tranquil waters of Chesapeake Bay, Maryland.

underneath them, then surfaced on the far side of the bay. The creature was dark brown, and had a humpback. Those who saw it said it was about 35 feet (10.5 m) long and 1 foot (30 cm) thick. But it was only showing part of its body, so it could have been longer.

The videotape shot by Robert Frew ran for three minutes. Scientists hoped that it might prove the sea serpent's existence. An important meeting of seven experts was held at the Smithsonian Institution, in Washington, D.C. However, the pictures on the tape were blurred. There was not enough detail for any conclusion to be reached.

A SEA GIANT

On the other side of the Atlantic, there have been many sightings of a sea monster off Falmouth, in Cornwall, England. It has appeared close inshore. In the old Cornish language, the monster has been named "Morgawr," which means sea giant. It was seen in 1876, and twice early in the 20th century. Then, in 1976, "Mary F." produced photographs.

She said the part of the beast she saw was about 15 to 18 feet (4.5 to 5.4 m) long. It looked "like an elephant waving its trunk. But the trunk was a long neck, with a small head on the end, like a snake's head." It seemed to be humpbacked. Its humps moved "in a funny way." Its skin was dark brown, or black, like a sea lion's. The photographs seemed genuine. But "Mary F." would not give her full name or address. Nor would she allow the negatives of the photos to be examined.

Since 1976, Morgawr has been sighted by many people. On July 10, 1985, author Sheila Bird was sitting on a cliff with her brother Eric, a scientist. Eric suddenly spotted a large, blotchy gray creature in the water below. It had a long neck, a small head, and its body was humpbacked. From high on the cliff, the pair could also see a long, muscled tail under the water. It was about the same length as the creature's body. The animal appeared to be nearly 20 feet (6 m) long. It held its head up high as it swam. Then it suddenly dived and disappeared.

SEA MONSTERS IN THE PACIFIC

Until late in the 19th century, there was little sea traffic in the Pacific Ocean. There were few tales of sea serpents. Also, there were no confirmed reports

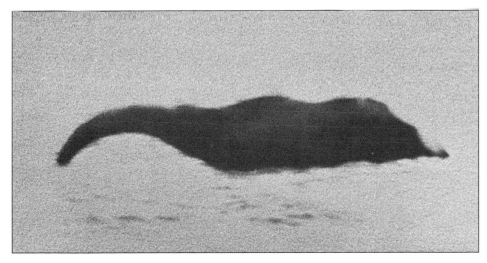

This photograph of Morgawr, the Cornish sea monster, was taken by "Mary F." in February 1976. Its long, slim neck and humpbacked body are clearly visible.

of monsters seen from the west coast of the United States until 1914. Then regular reports of a sea serpent began to come in. It had been seen swimming in the warm waters of the Outer Santa Barbara Channel, somewhere between the San Clemente and Santa Catalina islands, south of Los Angeles.

"I saw this great eel-like monster rear its head. Its eyes were red and green. . . ."

A. E. RICHARDS, FIRST OFFICER OF THE *SANTA LUCIA*

In 1920, Ralph Bandini, secretary of the Tuna Club, got a good look at it. It was truly a monster. Its head and neck rose 10 feet (3 m) out of the water. Bandini reckoned the neck was more than 5 feet (1.5 m) wide. The body was dark. It had a mane that looked like coarse hair. It also had huge, bulging eyes. Bandini thought that the monster was bigger than the largest whale.

Farther up the Pacific coast, near Vancouver in Canada, there was a monster known locally as "Caddy." This is short for Cadborosaurus. That name was jokingly given to it because it was most often seen in Cadboro Bay. On August 10, 1932, it was seen by F. W. Kemp, a local government official. It swam at amazing speed through the Strait of Georgia, between Vancouver Island and the British Columbia mainland.

In the following year, at dawn on October 21, 1933, the liner *Santa Lucia* was close to Cadboro Bay. First Officer A. E. Richards was on the bridge.

14

He reported: "I saw this great eel-like monster rear its head. Its eyes were red and green, like the port and starboard lights of a ship. It was about 90 feet [27 m] long. As we approached within 200 feet [60 m], it rose out of the water, with its seven humps like a camel, and its face like a cow. Then it gave an eerie [chilling] bellow—like a bull whale in its last agony—and reared up, perhaps 30 feet [9 m], perhaps 50 feet [15 m]. . . . By this time we had five searchlights on it, and it turned to the side and dived."

Caddy was seen often during the early 1930s. Then, on October 4, 1936, the skeleton of what was thought to be Caddy was found on some rocks off the coast of British Columbia. In spite of this, people in the area continued to report regular sightings of a monster resembling Caddy.

HUMPS AT SEA

On the afternoon of October 31, 1983, a road crew was repairing a stretch of U.S. Highway 1 in Marin County, California. The stretch where they were

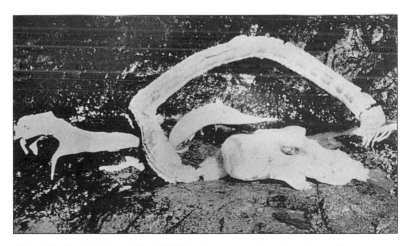

Was this the skeleton of Caddy? The bones were found on the rocks at Camp Fircom, off the coast of British Columbia, on October 4, 1936.

working runs along the coast north of San Francisco Bay. One of the crew, Matt Ratto, saw something very large traveling fast through the water toward the shore. It was a huge, dark animal. It was just a quarter of a mile (400 m) away. Ratto said it was 100 feet (30 m) long. But it was quite thin, "like a long black eel." He counted three humps. Then the creature turned and swam out to sea.

Truck driver Steve Bjora thought it moved at 45–50 miles per hour (mph) (72–80 kilometers per hour [kmph]). He saw only two humps. Altogether, five members of the construction crew saw the beast. They agreed on its appearance. Transportation safety inspector Marlene Martin also observed it. But she refused to talk about it. However, her daughter said her mother had told her she saw four humps. It was the largest thing she had ever seen.

This is San Francisco Bay. On October 31, 1983, many people witnessed a large beast traveling fast through the still waters toward the shore.

Three days later, a similar creature was seen. This time a group of surfers saw it. They were more than 400 miles (640 km) to the south, near Costa Mesa. Young Hutchinson described how it rose up out of the water. It was just off the Santa Ana River jetty. And that was only 10 feet (3 m) from his surfboard. He, too, said nothing at first. He thought "the whole thing was too crazy." Then he read about the Marin County sightings. His description was similar—a long, black eel.

PHOTOGRAPHIC EVIDENCE

Before the 1960s, nobody had taken a photograph of a sea monster. Until then, biologists had to rely on the descriptions of eyewitnesses. They really wanted to study a living creature, but a good picture would help. In 1965 a French photographer, Robert Le Serrec, claimed to have one.

On December 12, 1964, said Le Serrec, he was in a boat off the coast of Queensland, Australia. With him were his family and a friend named Henk de Jong. They were crossing the shallow waters of Stonehaven Bay. Suddenly Le Serrec's wife spotted something huge on the sandy seabed. It was only 6 feet (2 m) below. At first, the party thought it was a big, sunken tree trunk. Then, they realized it was an animal. It was shaped like an enormous tadpole. It had a big head and a long, tapering body.

Le Serrec took several photographs (see page 11). He moved closer. He began to film with his movie camera. Now the boat was nearer. The party could see the huge head more clearly. It was shaped like a snake's. Down the animal's back was a big wound, some 5 feet (1.5 m) long. The children in the boat

17

were frightened. They were taken back to shore. The adults went back to look at the monster. It did not move. So they guessed it was either dead or injured. They got even closer. They could see two white eyes on top of the head. There were bands of brown all along its black body.

"The monster began to move its jaws. It looked as if it was going to harm them."

Le Serrec later claimed he had a special camera with him to film the creature underwater. He and de Jong decided to dive near the animal for a closer look. But the water was cloudier than they thought. They had to swim to within 20 feet (6 m) of the beast. They judged its length to be about 75–80 feet (23–24 m). Its mouth was 4 feet (1 m) wide. The eyes were about 2 inches (5 cm) across. Now that Le Serrec and de Jong were close, they saw that the eyes were not white, but pale green. Le Serrec began filming. The monster began to move its jaws. It looked as if it was going to harm them. They quickly swam back to the boat. There Le Serrec's wife told them the monster had swum out to sea.

THE WORLD WONDERS

The Frenchman released his story on February 4, 1965. It created great excitement. However, there were some who refused to believe it. The photos seemed genuine. But few people were allowed to see the movies. It was rumored that they were blurred

18

and almost useless. Then some damaging facts about Le Serrec began to surface. He was wanted by the international police organization called Interpol.

In 1960 Le Serrec had left France, taking money he had been lent for an expedition. He told the people who lent him the money that he had an idea to make their fortune. He said the idea had "to do with a sea serpent." Le Serrec was arrested when he returned to France in 1966. He spent six months in jail. His photos appeared in the magazine *Paris Match*. But later, another publication revealed they had been a trick!

A decade later another photograph excited the scientists. On April 10, 1977, the fishing trawler *Zuiyo Maru* was off Christchurch, New Zealand. The crew found the body of a huge animal in one of their nets. It was decaying and stank. The crew was worried it would contaminate the catch of fish. They took photographs of it. It was also measured. The body was then thrown back into the sea. However, biologists later analyzed the information. They said the body was probably that of a large basking shark. Could all sea monsters simply be basking sharks or other fish?

A slightly fanciful drawing of a basking shark done in 1804. A similar creature could have been what the crew of Zuiyo Maru *caught in its nets in 1977.*

The Loch Ness Monster

"Nessie" is the most famous water monster in the world. But its identity remains a mystery.

There have been countless sightings of "Nessie," and many photographs have been shot. One of the best was taken by Jennifer Bruce in 1982 (opposite).

Loch Ness is a long, narrow lake in the Great Glen, which cuts like a deep canyon across the Highlands of Scotland. The loch is 22 miles (35 km) long. It is more than 970 feet (297 m) deep, but it is less than 1 mile (1.6 km) wide.

The first known sighting of the Loch Ness monster was 1,500 years ago. St. Columba had set up a monastery on the island of Iona, off Scotland's west coast. From there, he traveled through the north of Scotland. His task was to preach Christianity.

A LUCKY ESCAPE

In 565, St. Columba came to Loch Ness. One of his followers, called Lugne, was bold enough to swim across the mouth of the Ness River. He wanted to take a boat from the other side. Suddenly he met a "very odd looking beastie, something like a huge frog, only it was not a frog." The monster opened its mouth. It swam to attack Lugne.

Seeing this, St. Columba raised his arms and shouted: "Go thou no farther, nor touch the man. Go back at once!" Then, according to the account, "on hearing this word, the monster

"... it clearly showed a head and neck rising out of the water."

was terrified and fled away again. . . ."

In Scotland, the monster was called "Niseag." This is a Scottish Gaelic word. Its English name was "Nessie." For centuries, local people lived in fear of the monster. Children were told not to play near the water. There were hundreds of descriptions of the beast.

Patrick Rose reported, in 1771, that he had

St. Columba, who lived from 521 to 597, traveled through the north of Scotland preaching Christianity. In 565, he arrived at Loch Ness and saw the monster.

seen something in the loch. He described it as half like a horse, and half like a camel. In 1880, Duncan McDonald was trying to raise a sunken boat. "I was underwater about my work," he said, "when all of a sudden the monster swam by me as cool and calm as you please." In 1907, a group of children saw Nessie. She was slipping into the water. They said the monster had four legs. She was light brown in color. She looked "like a camel."

FRESH SIGHTINGS

For a few years, all seemed to be quiet. Then, on July 22, 1930, a man called Ian Milne was fishing for salmon with two friends.

They were in a small boat. Some 600 yards (546 m) away they suddenly saw spray being thrown high up into the air. A creature rushed toward them. It turned, then moved away again. It traveled at a speed of some 15 mph (24 kmph). "The part of it we saw would be about 20 feet [6 m] long. And it was standing 3 feet [60 cm] or so out of the water. The wash [waves] it created caused our boat to rock violently," reported Milne.

Until the 1930s the shores of Loch Ness were difficult to reach. Then, a new road was built along the north shore. Tourists began to arrive. Soon Nessie made the newspaper headlines. In spring, 1933, John Mackay and his wife told the *Inverness Courier* they had seen the monster for a minute or more. Mackay said the beast made the water "froth and foam." It had a very small head when compared to the size of its body.

Three months later, on July 22, George Spicer and his wife were driving along the new road. Their car nearly hit a huge black beast with a long neck. It waddled through the undergrowth. Then, it went into the water. Later the same year, on November 12, Hugh Gray was standing by the loch. He saw something large rise out of the water. So he took a photograph of it. He guessed it was 40 feet (12 m) long. He said it was gray, and had a very smooth, shiny skin.

Castle Urquhart once stood alone on the shores of Loch Ness. When a new road was built close by, tourists arrived—and sightings of Nessie began to increase.

This was the first photograph ever to have been taken of Nessie. It was printed in newspapers all over the world. However, it was very blurred.

The following year, on April 12, a clearer photograph appeared.

It was taken by a London physician, Colonel Robert Wilson. The picture showed a creature with a big body, a long neck, and a small head. Nessie looked like the ancient water reptile known as a plesiosaur.

STALKING THE MONSTER

Rewards were offered for the capture of Nessie. However, scientific experts were skeptical. At the British Museum, J. R. Norman stated: "The possibilities came down to the object being a bottlenose whale, one of the large species of shark, or just mere wreckage." He did not explain how a whale or shark could have gotten into Loch Ness.

World War II broke out in 1939. People had other things to think about. It was not until the 1950s that Nessie became news again. One of those who reported a sighting was David Slorach. He described it to *Harper's* magazine. On February 4, 1954, he was driving along the north shore of Loch Ness to Inverness. What he saw reminded him of "a cat with a long neck. One black floppy 'ear' fell

Hugh Gray took this photograph on November 12, 1933. It was the first photograph of Nessie, and it appeared in newspapers all over the world.

24

This is one of the clearest early photographs of Nessie. It was taken on April 12, 1934, by Colonel Robert Wilson. Experts say it resembles a plesiosaur—an ancient water reptile.

over where the eye might be, and four long black streaks ran down the 'neck.' The object was traveling through the water at great speed, throwing up a huge wave behind."

A special "Loch Ness Investigation Bureau" was set up. Then, in 1960 and 1967, the monster was caught on film. Both films were blurred, but showed a fast-moving object leaving a wave behind it as it shot through the water. Experts suggested that this was caused by an otter. But the object's length above the loch's surface was about 7 feet (2.1 m). This was much longer than any otter.

STRANGE SHAPES

On the evening of May 4, 1968, a number of people sighted what they thought was the monster. In August, a team from Birmingham University, England, set up a sonar scanner on a pier in Loch Ness. A sonar scanner is a machine that detects any sound made by moving objects. On August 28, they made a remarkable 13-minute recording.

A large object rose through the water from the bottom of the loch. It was about half a mile (800 m) away from them. It was traveling at a speed of around 100 feet (30 m) per minute, moving away from the pier. Then the object turned toward the pier again and dived deep. The sounds from a second object were recorded at the same time. This object dived at 450 feet (135 m) per minute.

". . . if there is a monster, or more than one, in Loch Ness, what can it be?"

The leader of the scientific team, Dr. Braithwaite, wrote that the rapid speeds that had been recorded for both objects made it unlikely that they were schools of fish, which had been one possible explanation. And in any case, biologists were unable to suggest what type of fish they might have been.

FILMING NESSIE

It was not until 1970 that underwater photography was tried. Because the water was murky, this was difficult. But there were some interesting results. Dr. Robert Rines, a scientific expert from Boston, Massachusetts, was one of the most successful. He took photographs that showed some kind of animal fin. Later, something that looked like a complete long-necked creature was photographed.

Above water, visitors to Loch Ness continued to produce photographs they claim are of the monster surfacing. One of the most convincing was taken by Jennifer Bruce in 1982. She took a picture of the view across part of the loch. At the time she noticed nothing unusual. But, when the photograph was developed, it clearly showed a head and neck rising out of the water.

A MYSTERIOUS IDENTITY

If there is a monster, or more than one, in Loch Ness, what can it be? Most descriptions are closest to that of a plesiosaur—a water reptile believed to have been extinct for the past 70 million years. Animals are said to be extinct, meaning that they have all died, once they have not been seen for a long time. But they may still exist. Until 1938, the coelacanth, a very ugly fish, was also said to have been extinct for 70 million years. Then fishermen started catching it in the Indian Ocean.

OPERATION DEEPSCAN

Nessielike monsters have also been reported in nearby lochs. Whatever these beasts are, teams of people continue to seek them. Between 1962 and 1977, six different groups of people used the most modern equipment to explore Loch Ness. They obtained results that could not be explained as being due to fish, nor anything like a sunken log.

Then, in 1987, came "Operation Deepscan." A fleet of motorboats, each equipped with sound-detecting equipment, swept the loch from end to end. But they found nothing. That was not really surprising. The boats filled the area with the noise of their engines. That would surely frighten any creature into hiding. So the search for Nessie continues.

In 1987, "Operation Deepscan" attempted to solve the Loch Ness mystery. However, the fleet of 24 boats failed to find any trace of Nessie.

The Lakes of North America

It is not just the lochs of Scotland that have monsters. The lakes of North America have them too!

One of the most famous lake monsters of North America is "Champ." It haunts Lake Champlain—a narrow lake like Loch Ness, but much longer. It runs for 109 miles (175 km) due south from the Canadian border, between New York State and Vermont.

The traditional story is that the monster was spotted in 1609 by French explorer Samuel de Champlain. The lake bears his name. But the first record of Champ's being seen was made in the summer of 1819. A boatman reported that he saw a huge creature with a long neck. It held its head 15 feet (4.5 m) above the water. At first, many people doubted the truth of the story. However, there have been some 250 sightings of Champ since then.

Lake Champlain (opposite) is 109 miles (175 km) long. It provides an enormous playground for "Champ," one of North America's most famous monsters.

THE DEFINITIVE DESCRIPTION

The first detailed description of the Champlain monster came in July 1883. It was given by Captain Nathan H. Mooney, the sheriff of Clinton County, New York. He was on the northwest shore of the lake when he saw an enormous "water serpent" rise out of the water. It was about 50 yards (46 m) away. Its head

"A boatman reported that he saw a huge creature with a long neck."

appeared 5 feet (1.5 m) above the rough waves. He figured that its neck was about 7 inches (18 cm) thick, and he put the full length of the body at 25–30 feet (8–9 m). He said the neck was curved, "like a goose when about to take flight." He could see strong muscles in the creature's neck. And he noted round white spots inside its mouth.

A STAR IS BORN

Numerous reports were made over many years. Then, in July 1981, the little village of Port Henry, New York, at the southern end of the lake, decided to exploit the fame of the monster. Buildings were painted apple green because the villagers had decided that this was the color of the monster. The names of 100 people who had sighted Champ were painted on a wooden billboard. This was posted at the entrance to Port Henry. Then pictures of a cartoon-like beast appeared in the shop windows and on signposts. There were even T-shirts and special buttons.

This drawing, from the book Historia Canadensis *(1664), is the monster Samuel de Champlain saw in the lake in 1609.*

In the late summer of 1981, the *New York Times* printed a photograph taken four years earlier by Mrs. Sandra Mansi of Connecticut. It showed a dark body, with a long neck lifted clear of the water. Mrs. Mansi said she thought it looked "like a dinosaur." The photograph appeared to be real. Sadly the negative has been lost.

Monsters have been seen in other lakes: Flathead Lake, Montana; Lake Walker, Nevada; Lake Folsom, California; Bear Lake, Utah; and Lake Payette, Idaho.

Lake Payette, Idaho, is home to Slimy Slim. The monster has been spotted at different times by more than 30 people.

In July and August 1941, "Slimy Slim" was spotted in Lake Payette by more than 30 different people. For a time afterward, nobody reported the sightings. Then Thomas L. Rogers, city auditor from Boise, Idaho, spoke to a local newspaper reporter.

Rogers said the serpent was about 50 feet (15 m) long. It moved with a wavy motion at about 5 mph (8 kmph). He said its head was like that of a snubnosed crocodile. It was about 8 inches (20 cm) above the water. He figured the total length of the body at about 35 feet (10.5 m). The story of Slimy Slim was published in *Time* magazine, but after that little was seen or heard of it again.

CANADIAN MONSTERS

There are said to be monsters in many of the lakes of the St. Lawrence River valley, north of the Canadian border. Lake Pohénégamook, in Quebec, close by the border with Maine, has its "Ponik." The town of Saint-Eleuthére, at the head of the lake, holds a regular "Ponik festival." Sightings have been reported since 1873.

Father Calixte Bérubé, a priest, has described what he and 15 other people saw one afternoon. "From the path, we had a magnificent view of the lake. We saw the back with its fin. It frolicked like a fish and shimmered in the sun." In the mid–1970s, three divers spent 10 days searching for Ponik. They took a picture of a dark shape some 25 feet (8 m) long.

Farther south, crossing from Canada into the state of Maine, lies Lake Memphremagog. This is another narrow lake some 50 miles (80 km) long.

On October 26, 1935, Dr. Curtis Classen, from Brooklyn, New York, was staying at his vacation home beside the lake. His back was to the water when he sensed something staring at him. Turning,

"It frolicked like a fish and shimmered in the sun."

FATHER CALIXTE BÉRUBÉ

he saw a creature like a large alligator. It was climbing onto the bank. He ran to bring his wife and a friend. They were just in time to see the creature crawling back into the water. There were large pawprints on the sandy shore.

In a letter written later, Dr. Classen said: "We estimated [guessed] that the creature was 18 inches [46 cm] wide and 10 feet [3 m] long." In October 1937, John Webster also saw prints on the same beach. He figured the animal that left them had been about 20 inches (51 cm) wide and 11 feet (3 m) long. In 1966 or 1967, Hank Dewey was fishing on the lake with two women passengers. Suddenly "a big fish, but it did not look like a fish," appeared near the bank. "The women were so frightened that they never again went on the lake."

SCALED TERROR

A very different description of the monster of Lake Memphremagog was given in 1972. It was about 10:00 P.M. on a clear night. Mrs. Helen Hicks was in a small boat with an outboard motor. A spotlight from the boat fell on the creature. Mrs. Hicks said the creature was about 75–100 feet (23–30 m) long. It had a round body. Its head was like that of a horse, with two red eyes. The neck was long. And the back appeared to be covered with large scales. "It started to come for the boat. It rolled over near the boat, causing it to be very tippy. It shorted out the boat motor."

Some experts believe many of the monsters of the Canadian lakes are really giant sturgeons. These fish, they say, can grow up to 12 feet (3.6 m) long. But the monsters could also be a type of dinosaur—the lakes of Canada and Alaska are left over from the last ice age. Perhaps there are all sorts of creatures, trapped in the water, that have yet to be discovered.

THE SNAKE IN THE LAKE

Of all the North American monsters, the most famous is probably Ogopogo. This monster is said to inhabit Lake Okanagan, a long, deep, mountain lake in British Columbia. Native Americans told

Although this may look like a monster, it is not! It is a giant sturgeon that lives in the fresh waters of some Canadian lakes. Many experts believe that this is what people have seen when they claim to have spotted a monster.

33

tales of Naitaka, "snake of the water." When they had to cross the lake, they would throw in live animals to satisfy it.

In the 1850s, John MacDougall was crossing Lake Okanagan in his canoe. Two horses were swimming behind on ropes. He forgot about the monster, and the need to feed it. Suddenly, something began to pull a horse down. It would have dragged the canoe under. But MacDougall cut the ropes with his knife, leaving the horses to their fate.

OGOPOGO REVEALS ITSELF

In July 1890, Captain Thomas Shorts, of the steamer *Jubilee*, saw a creature some 15 feet (4.5 m) long. It had a head like a ram. The sun shone through its fins. This was the first reported sighting. Soon there were others. They continued year after year.

In the summer of 1952, a woman visitor from Vancouver saw the monster. It was swimming just a couple of hundred yards away. She said later: "I am a stranger here. I didn't even know such things existed. But I saw it so plainly. A head like a cow, or a horse, that reared right out of the water. It was a wonderful sight. The coils glistened like two huge wheels. There were ragged edges along its back, like a saw. It was so beautiful, with the sun shining on it."

In August 1968, Art Folden and his wife were driving home along the shore of the lake. They suddenly noticed something moving in the water. It

A model of Ogopogo (Lake Okanagan's monster) at Kelowna, British Columbia.

was about 300 yards (273 m) away. Folden had a small movie camera with him. It was loaded with color film and had a telephoto lens. He had been using it to film the day's outing. Fortunately there were a few feet of film left.

Folden shot film for about one minute, in short bursts. He photographed the object only when it was visible on the surface. This was an important sighting. But Folden kept quiet about it. He showed his film only to friends and relatives. Then, in February 1970, his brother-in-law persuaded him to show it to other people. It caused a sensation.

Judging from the size of the pine trees in the foreground, the creature was about 60 feet (18 m) long, and 3 feet (90 cm) wide. It moved very fast and left a clear wake. Some people thought they could see a head and tail. Others were not so sure. However, local author Arlene Gaal was convinced by the film. She had studied the Ogopogo reports for years. In 1981 she herself took a photograph of something she believed was the monster.

WAS IT A BEAVER?

In 1989 Ken Chaplin shot a video of something moving through the water. He described it as a dark green, snakelike creature. He said it was about 15 feet (4.5 m) long. Wildlife experts were shown the video. However, they thought the animal was more likely a beaver, or a large otter.

Hunting guide Ernie Giroux saw a creature close to the same spot. Giroux was told what the experts had made of Chaplin's video. "I've seen a lot of animals swimming in the wild," he said, "and what we saw that night was definitely not a beaver."

35

Lakes Around the World

There are lakes the world over. And many are home to strange creatures.

One of the first tales of lake monsters in South America was told by Father Juan-Ignacio Molina. In his *Essay on the Natural History of Chile*, published in 1782, he wrote that the natives of Chile reported "a fish or dragon of monstrous size." They called it the "fox-serpent." They believed it ate people, so they never swam in the lakes where it lived.

SUMMER SIGHTINGS

Close to Chile, in the Andean mountains of southern Argentina, lies Lake Nahuel Huapi. It covers 380 square miles (984 sq km). Here a monster has been seen by many visitors, as well as by local people. Nicknamed "Nahuelito," it seems to surface only in summer. That may be because summer is the tourist season.

Nahuelito appears when the lake is calm. There is a sudden swell and a shooting spray of water. Descriptions of the creature vary greatly. Its length has been said to be anything from 15 to 150 feet (4.5 to 45 m). Some witnesses have reported a giant water snake with humps, and fins like a fish. Others describe it as "a swan with a snake's head."

An approaching storm whips up the waters of Lake Nahuel Huapi (opposite) in Argentina. It is only during the summer months that its monster, "Nahuelito," makes an appearance.

36

"'Nahuelito' appears when the lake is calm. There is a sudden swell and a shooting spray of water."

On the other side of the world, in the African Republic of Congo, people tell stories of monsters called mokele-mbembe. These are terrifying creatures, the size of a hippopotamus. But the mokele-mbembe has a long neck and tail, and clawed feet. It is said to attack canoes, killing all aboard.

PREHISTORIC LANDSCAPE

Scientist Roy Mackal decided to brave the danger. In 1980 and 1981 he mounted searches for the monster. The explorers plunged into the Likouala swamp. This is a huge, almost unexplored area of the Republic of Congo, on the border with the Central African Republic. Crammed into a dugout canoe, the party searched the waterways of the swamp. It was like parts of the world had been when the dinosaurs roamed, millions of years ago. Perhaps mokele-mbembe was a survivor from those times.

An officer of the Congolese Army told Mackal that the creature dug caves in the banks of the waterways.

Mackal was shown mokele-mbembe's footprint. But he was forced to admit that this might have been made by an elephant. And as for the creature itself, there was not a trace.

Throughout parts of Europe there are many reports of a monster known as a "water-horse." This

This painting of mokele-mbembe was based on eyewitness descriptions of those who had seen the monster in Africa.

comes out from a lake or river. Then, according to legend, it carries men, women, and children away. People in the U.S. and Canada have also reported monsters with a mane, or a head like a horse. It seems likely that they are describing a similar animal.

NORTHERN EUROPE

One of these monsters is said to live in Lake Storsjön, in central Sweden. It has been reported for more than 350 years. A century ago, a scientist named Dr. Peter Olsson spent many years following up sightings. The beast was red, with a white mane. It

In the 1970s, a huge trap (above) was made in Sweden. It was baited with baby pigs. Then it was put beside Lake Storsjön. But the monster did not take the bait.

moved very fast, at a speed of some 45 mph (72 kmph). Since 1987, nearly 500 different sightings have been recorded. Some witnesses have described a beast with a long neck. The movement of its neck looks like the waving of a horse's mane. Others reported that the creature was like a giant worm. But it had ears on its head. Estimates of its length vary from 10–45 feet (3–14 m).

Iceland also has its monster. English author Reverend Sabine Baring-Gould visited that country in 1860. He was told about the monster "Skrimsl." It lived in the lake called Lagarfljot. The monster was 50 feet (15 m) long. In Norway, he heard about a similar creature in Lake Suidal. Its head was said to be as big as a rowboat. More than a century later, in August 1986, Aasmund Skori observed something in Norway's Lake Seljord. The water was calm, and he saw a sort of "bow" emerge. "The bow was one and a half meters [5 feet] long," he said, "as thick as a thigh, and looked black. The body divided the water in front. Behind it the lake was frothing."

"The monster looked like a horse. But it had big eyes and a forked tail."

THE WATER-HORSE IN IRELAND

The greatest number of stories about the "water-horse" come from Ireland. The name usually given to the beast in Irish is "peiste." One of the earliest descriptions is in the 10th century *Book of Lismore*. The monster looked like a horse. But it had big eyes and a forked tail. The 12th century *Book of the Dun Cow* tells of a peiste living in the deep lake of Slieve Mis, in County Kerry. It would come out of the water to seize cattle.

In the 19th and 20th centuries, monsters were reported from a number of the lakes of Connemara, in County Galway. As in Canada, these lakes were formed at the end of the last ice age. There are hundreds of these lakes—known in Ireland as "loughs" —dotted all over the land.

On February 22, 1968, farmer Stephen Coyne was on the shores of Lough Nahooin. He saw something black in the water. He thought it was his dog. So he whistled. The shape in the water did not respond.

Then, to his surprise, his dog came running up to him from behind. When it saw the creature in the lough, it began barking.

Coyne was joined by his wife and children. They watched the monster for some time, until the light faded. It came to within 30 feet (9 m) of them. It was about 12 feet (4 m) long. It had a smooth skin, like an eel. Its neck was 12 inches (30 cm) in diameter. The inside of its mouth was pale. When the monster put its head under the water, two humps appeared above the surface. They also saw its tail.

LEAVING THE WATER

Most of the great lakes where monsters have been reported—such as Lake Nahuel Huapi--are huge. But most of the loughs in Connemara are very small. There is not enough food in any one lough for a huge creature to live on. However, a creature might survive by leaving the water to seek food.

On September 8, 1968, farmer Thomas Connelly saw a black creature, "bigger than a young donkey," on the shore of Lough Nahooin. This lough is only 300 feet (91 m) long and 240 feet (73 m) wide. The black creature had four stumpy legs. It crept back into the water. If beasts such as this can move on dry land, then it would be possible for them to travel from one lough to another in search of food.

Monster hunting on Lough Nahooin in 1968. On the right is Roy Mackal, the U.S. scientist who later led the search for mokele-mbembe in Africa.

Looking at the Evidence

Mistaken identity probably accounts for most reported water monsters. But what about the rest?

Reports of monsters all around the world have created a new word—"cryptozoologist." The "crypto" part of the word means "hidden," and zoologists study animals. So cryptozoologists try to make sense of reports of animals unknown to everyday science.

One man, in particular, has spent many years analyzing the accounts of sea monsters. He is Dr. Bernard Heuvelmans, a Belgian zoologist. In 1965, he published his book *In the Wake of the Sea Serpents*. Here he listed studies of 587 events. The reports dated from 1639 to 1964.

SORTING THE SIGHTINGS

Out of his total of 587, Heuvelmans found 56 to be pretended sightings, or tricks. He decided that another 52 were sightings of known sea creatures—such as the giant squid. These creatures had been mistakenly described as unknown monsters. He put aside another 121 reports—the detail was too confused.

This left 358 sightings that Heuvelmans felt were real. He found that these could be divided into nine different types of animals: the long-necked; the merhorse (sea horse); the

The plesiosaur (opposite) is an ancient water reptile that existed when dinosaurs roamed the Earth over 150 million years ago.

"The descriptions of these creatures are like the prehistoric plesiosaur."

many-humped; the many-finned; the super-otter; the super-eel; the marine saurian (a reptile); the father-of-all-turtles; and the yellow-belly.

The creature most often reported is the long-necked sea serpent. The merhorse (sea horse) has a different-shaped head, more like that of a horse. It has big eyes and a red mane. The many-humped sea serpent and the super-otter are about the

The largest known species of turtle is the leatherback, which can measure 12 feet (4 m) across. It is possible that larger turtles exist.

same size, 60–100 feet (18–30 m) long. The many-humped serpent is the one that is most often seen along the coast of New England. It swims with a single pair of large fins. It also has a "forked" tail, like that of a shark. The super-otter has a thicker neck and a bigger head. It has a pair of big paws in front, and a pair of smaller paws, or fins, farther back.

FIGHTING FOR LIFE

Heuvelmans believed that the super-otter had not been sighted since 1848. He believed it was now extinct. He suggested that the long-necked sea serpent and the super-otter were competitors, and that the super-otter had probably lost the battle for survival. The many-finned monster grows to 60 feet (18 m) or more in length. It blows a spray of water from its nostrils, like a surfacing whale. It has only been sighted in tropical waters.

Heuvelmans believes the first five types of monsters are mammals. The super-eel is more likely to be a fish. It normally lives deep in the ocean. It only comes to the surface when it is near death. The marine saurian is a reptile. It looks like a crocodile and has been seen only in tropical waters. It is 50–60 feet (15–18 m) long. It might be a survivor from Jurassic times, when dinosaurs roamed the earth more than 150 million years ago.

HARDY SURVIVORS

Turtles have been around for some 175 million years. The largest known type of turtle, called the Atlantic leatherback, can weigh more than three-quarters of a ton. It measures 12 feet (4 m) across. So it is possible that an animal like the "father-of-all-turtles" still lives in the warm tropical depths.

The "yellow-belly" is the most difficult to explain. There are few detailed descriptions. It may be a huge fish or an unknown species of shark.

Other cryptozoologists have made different suggestions. One of these is that the sea serpent is an unknown giant species, similar to the long-necked leopard seal of the Antarctic. Another is that it is a primitive or early type of whale called a zeuglodon, which is supposed to be extinct.

Many experts believe that the sea serpent could be a giant relation of the long-necked leopard seal that is found in the Antarctic (above).

PREHISTORIC ORIGINS

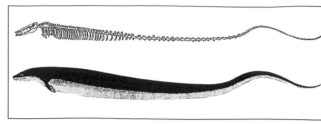

The zeuglodon is a primitive whale thought to have died out 50 million years ago. Perhaps the lake monsters "Champ," "Caddy," and "Ogopogo" are its survivors.

Many descriptions of water monsters sound like the prehistoric plesiosaur. However, most reports of such sightings are from the 20th century. Today most people know what prehistoric dinosaurs looked like. One description of a monster could well be a description of a plesiosaur. It looked like "a snake that had swallowed a barrel." But experts believe that the plesiosaur moved very slowly. Besides, its neck was not flexible. It could not move in the way witnesses have described.

Those who do not believe in water monsters have many explanations to offer. The most popular is that the "humps" of a sea serpent, moving fast through the sea, are really a line of porpoises jumping out of the water, one behind the other. And it has been suggested that the Loch Ness sightings are of a number of salmon, doing the same thing.

A BASIC EXPLANATION

Many people think that water monsters are nothing more than floating tree trunks. But this does not account for the rapid movement that so many witnesses report. Nothing will be known for sure until a monster is captured.

Huge areas of the Earth's surface remain largely unexplored. Many of these areas are in the oceans. Every year a thousand or more new species of living creatures are identified. Who knows when a new monster may emerge from the deep?

Glossary

archbishop An important priest in the Christian church.

biologists People who study biology, which is the science of living things.

bulging Swelling where you would expect something to be flat.

confirm (ed) To support or prove that something is correct.

contaminate To pollute or infect, or to make radioactive.

estimated The roughly worked out size, length, weight, or volume of something.

existence To be living, or real, rather than something from the imagination or in a story.

extinct No longer alive, active, or in existence.

fanciful Something from the imagination, often unrealistic.

ice age A time when Earth was covered with ice. There have been several ice ages in Earth's history.

incident A specific event.

jetty A platform built out into the water. Used for getting on and off boats, or to protect against the sea.

kmph Kilometers per hour.

mollusks Small creatures with no backbone. They have a soft body, and a hard shell—like a snail.

monstrous Enormous or huge, sometimes terrifying or bizarre.

mph Miles per hour.

naturalist A person who studies wildlife—animals and plants.

prehistoric Before humans began to keep written historical records.

resemble To look like, or behave like, something or somebody else.

skeptical To be unwilling to believe a claim or promise made by somebody else.

sonar scan A machine that detects sounds made by moving objects.

species Groups of plants or animals that have common features.

squids Sea creatures with long, soft bodies and 10 tentacles, or arms. An octopus has eight arms.

tapering Gradually narrowing.

trawler A type of boat that is used to catch fish at sea. Fish are caught in a trawl, a large bag-shaped net.

undergrowth The thick growth of bushes, shrubs, and other plants under trees in a wood or forest.

zoologist A person who studies zoology, the science of animals.

47

Index

Further Reading

Collard, Sneed B. *Sea Snakes.* Boyds Mills Press, 1997

Garcia, Eulalia. *Giant Squid: Monsters of the Deep*, "Secrets of the Animal World" series. Gareth Stevens, 1997

Landau, Elaine. *The Loch Ness Monster*, "Mysteries of Science" series. Millbrook Press, 1993

Ross, Stewart. *Monsters of the Deep*, "Fact or Fiction" series. Millbrook Press, 1997